hooligan trees

hooligan trees

alan burke

the bad press

First published in 2000
by The Bad Press,
 PO Box 76,
Manchester, M21 8HJ.
www.thebadpress.co.uk

ISBN 1 903160 02 2

1 3 5 7 9 2 4 6 8

Cover designed by Robert Cochrane.
Cover illustration by Gilbert and George.
Author as a child copyright Lynn Taylor.
Author photo 1998 by Lynn Taylor.
Book edited by Robert Cochrane.

Printed by
The Arc and Throstle Press Limited,
Nanholme Mill, Shaw Wood Road,
Todmorden, Lancs, OL14 6DA.

Distributed by
Turnaround Ltd,
27 Horsell Road,
London N5 1XL.

CONTENTS

INTRODUCTION

Alan Burke is a fantastic poet.
His early death was a tragedy.
When we met him we thought him
lovely looking, serious, intense
and clearly very talented.
The publication of his poems
will give us all a chance
to feel his world and soul.
We love his poetry very much.

Gilbert and George
London
9th November 1999

For Lynn Taylor

VISION

I'm so sick of having eyes!
Everywhere,
At everything I look,
I see,
Glazing back at me,
Cookie faced thief child
Pictures.
They hound me,
Another Nemesis
Obstinately refusing to
Piss off back
To where they came from.

Why does Earth worship the eye
So much?
Why can't there just be somewhere
Blank,
Bland -
A black leather boot kick at vision?

THE MANNISH TREE

The mannish tree
Weighed down to the ground
By peared air,
Providing shade for the
Termites and bugs.

The mannish trees
Branches -
New worlds for local
Children to
Explore and conquer.

The mannish tree,
A grimy slur on the air
In front of the new factory.

The mannish tree,
A log of
Paper pulp or
Fire fuel.
A womanish squeal as it is
Bulldozed to death.

THE LONER'S LOVE

Loners make the best lovers.
They chisel out an Ionic pedestal
From their wildest expectations
And lay on its top, on a
Gushing bed of
Bubble wrap, the
Bog-standard concept -
Love.

With regularity, this idea they
Inject with 10 ml. of
100% proof Dream,
Till
Butterfly like a
Paragon bursts forth
Fully fledged
From its chrysalis
And flutters
Serenely around the brain.

But the vat of
Rampant bubbling Dream
Can't be guarded by
The soldiers of moderation
Twenty-four hours a day -
Sleep invades their eyes
Allowing the Butterfly
To plop into the liquid.

It emerges as a
Wizard's wildest fantasy,

A pterodactyl on steroids,
Flapping its wings against
The air's cowering body.

The loner's brain stands
Helpless
Before its own creation,
Before this
Life gorged on zest,
Before this dream
Which swallows its creator.

RAILWAY BOY

Knotted to his father's ropey
Arm, the lad is
Tied to his life so tight it's
Choking!
Though a tumour or a car-bonnet
Ten years hence has his Death's
Name ingrained on to it,
This second is his
Rich sea to sail in
Whichever ramshackle
Pile he puts in the water.

By the time they come to
Their counter,
He's already forgotten his
Previous ten-minute
Long wait-journey -
He's reached the Bermudas
From the Cape of Good Hope
Without so much as being
Splashed by a drop of water.
But he does hold aloft,
Over his freckled face,
The winner's golden plate
For ten whole, long minutes
Pounded out from
Its ore into
His journey.

After receiving
Reservation tickets,
They shuffle out into their

Future -
A spread-eagle Goddess,
Ready for them both to
Enter.

I follow their lives out the door
With my rapacious eyes,
Get my ticket
And walk off.

SUN GOD

The Sun thinks it's
 God-All-Bloody-Mighty,
Creator of Heaven and Earth
Mercifully dishing out
A stray morsel of light-beam
To a cotton white
Tom-cat Earth,
Lapping it up.

How I would love to
Throttle its screaming neck,
How I would love to bury its
Big fat belly under the
Darkest Elm tree
Late one night.

Then we would see
Who was God!

APHRODITE'S ERROR

Ares walked by Aphrodite
One day as she was busy
Working out beauty quotas
On her Lap-Top,
Ooooo, those legs!!!
She hit the wrong number.

Thus here you are a fairer form
God's mind couldn't mould.

Your burning hair sets alight the paper night.
        Ahh, such beauty,
Your face is sweeter than Love.
        Ahh, such beauty,

Your eyes are orgies of erupting emeralds.
        Ahh, such beauty,
Your arms are two paths to the Elysian Fields.
        Ahh, such beauty,

Your stomach is a silken bed on which sprawls Eternity.
        Ahh, such beauty,
Your legs were carved from white marble.
        Ahh such beauty.

Paris would have stolen one of your toe-nail clippings
With the same eagerness he swiped up Helena!
        Such is your beauty.
What a shame this beauty is not mine.

PERFECTION

I saw you and
Instantly lost
My belief in God -
No God who wished to
Remain sane would allow
An equal perfection
To come into being.
I saw you -
A retina exploding blaze
Of brilliant perfection -
Opposite me,
And knew your face had
Seized my future,
Knew that I had found
The consummation of my existence.

I touched your lips
And felt the warmth of
Eden's sun on my soul,
And from then on
We were nailed
To each other's cross.

The word 'love' was a
Scrawny goblin we'd keep locked up
So monstrously inadequate was
It as an articulation
Of our feelings...
Every blink,

Every breath,
Every thought
Of mine was more
Worthy an expression of my worship
Of you than any
Disgraceful word would be.

Then you left me.
All I could do was cry.
The foundations were
Blown from under my Spirit,
The Universe tried to console me
By saying it would wear
Black until its dying day
To mark the ending of
Its greatest union...

Forgive me for having to say
These awful words over your
Grave.

THE RAVEN

The demon-stone
Perched on top of the lamp-post,
Its beady eyes
Black rubies
Igniting its frenzied face
To a frazzle,
As its every greasy feather
Fans the flames of its
Combustion.

The darkness billowing
From its body,
Whirling the sky.
The goodness of the Earth
Kneeling at the foot of the
Lamp-post
For ever having dared to be.

A grotesque squawk
Retched up from its
Stomach guts,
Attacks the mousy air.
The audible blackness,
Chilling.

I fasten my woollen coat,
I am a stray lamb
Soon to be

Engulfed by its
Sweeping spiky beak.
hurrying on
I feel my neck skin
Being chewed off
Before having it spat back
On my head.
Only then, it allows me to hurry on
My journey.

MEAL FOR ONE

How I need to love
But I'm just too scared,
Therefore let me die
And I'll court Angels instead.

My heart sniggers at me continually
And screams as I try to sleep -
How I'd love to silence it
By falling in love deep.

A meal for one I buy
And at table stiffly sit,
Silence howls all around
In the cafe dimply lit.

The world processes me rapidly
As I give it a little smile,
Much too busy it is
To talk with me a while.

My spirit begs a partner,
My heart leaves after a row,
I don't care about such things,
I get used to everything now.

THE PARK

The day wrapped around
The sun, like a duffel coat
Steaming,
Pulsating
A Sicilian bull of a one,
Laying the air
Around like freshly stoked bricks,
Bringing all the world to the park.
Here are the
White skinned beer-guts,
Clothes plummeting off their
Bodily cliffs
To show small brown hairs,
Little moles shoving their
Heads out to survey the area.
Here are the lovers
With kissing eyes,
Their souls
Joined at the heart.
So young, yet so in love.
Here are the children
Insanely
Pelting for the second
Like rabid dogs
Slowly barking out their
Innards -
The only nip on the day's
Silent sleet.

And there is the occasional
Foolhardy bird
Pulling up its
Feathery dress and
Scuffling over the
Hot coal sky
Ooo-ahhing all the way.

But razorish Time has
Slit the day's wrists
And it is bleeding,
Becoming
Anaemic.

TERRACE

Look down the terrace -
Children, lungs of the day,
Licking air like a lolly
Bouncing on the hour's inflatable pulse,
Their eyesight spraying around like a frenzied hose,
As they teach the pigeons the ways of soccer
Whilst fold armed mothers at the door
Are hauled in on gossipy looks.
O happy terrace.

"Quick I say, Hurry..."
The day must be forced indoors
With the children, dogs and gossip
For it is Come
Among the smiled skinned breeze,
Litter takes on the mantle
Of the children's play
Hoppinghoppingsadlyaround
The sunken contours of a speedily removed day,
Eyes quivering like cornered adders
From the edges of upstairs windows
Of the terrace.

THE TUMOUR CLOUD

A throbbing sun,
A sweating day,
As summer is released to
Cheering crowds from its
Spring-time cell.
The atmosphere's megaphones
Oozing a
Cool
Jazz tune,
And the sky
Empty but for two
Attempts at clouds.
But also a distant
Black tumourous cloud -
At the moment quiet,
Unnoticed and harmless,
But insidiously swelling,
Angio-genesis,
Sucking rain and birds,
Clouds and sky into its
Cavernous belly
Till it bursts...
Metastic sprinkling
Around the sky
Which crumples suddenly
To its knees,
Squealing as it
Dissolves into rain.

THE HEAD-ACHES

My head,
Empty as a cave, urging to
Enter every hobo-headache
Which needs to rest its weary body.
But they refuse to lie down on
Such comfortable mattresses
And silken sheets,
But clatter around, invading hordes,
Starting fires, shuffling rocks
Until my mind crumbles at the seams.
Every mouth chews my silence,
A succulent cream-bun,
Dribbling and burping out
The sweetest bits
Until I shake my skull
to try and dislodge them,
But I only succeed in making
Clutch to my neurons
Like a group of filthy Tarzans.
I peer onto the mirror
At my vibrating head,
Their trampoline,
A free-entry amusement park
For all who can squeeze in.
Furious, I whisk up my bottle of pills
And pop one after the other -
I feel them getting tired,
For the time being.

ANTS

An
Ant
Draws from me
The same awe
As would a tour of God's brain -
How could I not be amazed
At such soul destroying beauty
Contained in such a speck of life?
Not necessarily physical beauty
But the beauty of being a living nothing,
And to want nothing more than that,
To be content in its
Five metre squared planet,
Eating and reproducing
The only impulses which dare
Come into its brain,
And to spend the rest of
The time doing odd jobs
And lazing like cows!
And then some gigantic foot
Comes along and squashes you!
Your nothing becomes
A greater nothing.
Unmissed, unmourned,
Another nothing is born
And takes your place,
I think the beautiful ant
Leads the life man was meant to.

INSTANTS TERRAIN

Look out across the Instants terrain
View the world from that higher plain,
Take its sky in your hands
Count the grains of the stretching sands
Show that you master your own lands.
Then stride through the conquered day
Flicking mountains out the way
Urge to come All that may
Good or bad, gold or grey.

THE INVASION

I once got a splinter in my Spirit,
Agony lashed on its paper thin soles.
That must be the origin of the invasion.
I suppose it was just a matter of waiting after that.
A kind of cinder expectancy showered with tinder
Imminence to produce the Explosion.
The invaders organise,
Bustle bursting at the seams.
Tomorrow curls up with ration of beer
And thinks of battles to come.

The army fills a spineless body
Which won't stand up for me,
But buys traitorhood at a bargain price from the enemy.
Resilience is hauled on its gravel carved buttocks
And made to gaze upon his own alarms burning red
In a territory of stoneless walls and moss cloaked castles.
He extends two shattered hands as dams against the sea.

Binoculars saved Hope.
His family and the rest of the village
Were sentenced to life without parole in death's cells
By the kangaroo court established to dispose of them.
Eyes concreted in condemnation,
Hope glares to his collapsing life.
A broken tear, falls.
He runs to the vibrant hills,
Here he can musculise
The puny body of Resistance.

The invasion progresses unstoppable -
To conquer a coward isn't exacting.
Slag cowardice beds Effort -
The opposition falls,
O that unconquerable confidence of the conqueror.
Back in the hills, Hope sweats over logistics
And occasionally ambushes a lost Hun.
Eventually, off he goes,
Hope the guerrilla
Nipping (violently)
The leg of a colossus!

The mean phallus of Defeat enters fair Victory.
From the choking grip of despondence, Hope
Wiggles free to the cuddle of Annihilation.
In the camp, in a cell he is kicked
Screaming into pain by furious feet,
Then allowed a bite to eat.
The next hour sees him before the kangaroo court
Who speedily don black caps.
Shackled inside a day-dream,
The prisoner is led to a courtyard
And shot through with death.

CLOCKS

The alarm clock,
Egging on my finale,
Its jagged ticking
Ripping my brain to shards.
Growing in its arrogance,
Getting louder and louder
Pulsating the silent room,
Pancake-flat.

I desperately chuck
A cloth onto the clock,
But it sizzles from this cover
And buzzes around me,
Tsetse flies sucking at
My neck, hands and feet
Till its tickers are
Just flying melons.

Three rooms away
I can hear my kitchen clock
In cahoots with the Alarm clock.
Their dictatorial grip
On my head,
Unstoppable.

Until all places,
Clock ticking,
Ragged wailing
For my finale.

My mind oozes from
My ears and nostrils
Unutterable bleed.

I drop to my knees
Writhing my hair
From their damn roots,
Sobbing.

HIM

The pavement smeared with slow people
being stamped further into the concrete
by herds of padlocked feet,
as I clamber over tepid piles of deaded journey
sucking cannibalistically
at my ankles squeezing through those
on a vapid movement to the Hellism of the brain
swaying violently to the breaths of passers-by.

They carefully shout about him,
I pause to see their catatonic sensitivity
as one or two fart a coin into his cap.
Such a rippling mountain whose tattered
garments spray around like swooping hawks,
this pavement prince sprawled upon his regal bed
befilthed with dog excrement,
providing a nerving view

I glaze furiously intrigued to his majesty, This spectre
as his stinking, shoeless foot convulses in movement,
He speaks,
such a muscular voice,
breaking out in fine sweats
his transparent eyes maintain
the sinews of existence, my existence,
so I fire a spit at his face and leave.

All docile day he burgles my brain, stealing back
that image of his eyes until no more than nothing

remains as the gammy-legged moon heaves up
against a prop, those sugary eyes beckon me lick.
So to his starred chamber I go, Manoeuvring
those standing solid who
failed the journey, Dodging
a bunion footed wind loitering around
with the night time women...

...just a slimy purple sleeping bag crumpled into a ball
frames my view of the Destitute Kingdom,
peeling open I howl for the vanished Emperor
and in retaliation
carefully piss over his home.

HOOLIGAN TREES

Hooligan Trees
Rioting the distance,
Scuffles shuffles,
Tearing out clumps
Of each other's leaves
Before turning collective
Rage on their jailer - Nature,
Who flees to seek back up.

Tied between
A thousand twanging boughs,
Calmness is torn limb from limb,
Its wails but whispers
Amongst the tumultuous tumour of fury.

Their roar seems unstoppable -
Silence chooses to become a quisling -
Everywhere, noise Is the conqueror.

Then, like a sly Sioux,
Nature returns
Crawling through the tall grass,
Reinforcements with the wind.
Which is unleashed at the mob,
The fight lasts hours until beaten,
The trees surrender back to Nature's rule.
They settle once more into their treeness -
Meek, dopey, boring.

VIEWERS

Contained in my cell waiting on nothing
But a solution to present itself as
Reward for the ages I have spent
Pondering on...things...thoughts.

A snapped wall allows a glance of that
Other world flickering on and off
As a lighthouse guiding distressed vessels to it
During the storm.

The burning stink of colour,
The grizzled and tanned ships
Limping through the mists...
But Oh! how dangerous,
Oh! best I was here, safe,
Thinking and talking to myself about my self.

Time saturates into my cell, draining out via
The window which has grown out of that Damned snap,
I see Them... the hyenaism of man, laughing,
Looking, whispering, another Pompey's Porch

Viewing me from fourth-century mosaical eyes,
Weighing me in the thoughts of those eyes,
Living prosthetic abstractions
Stroking my brain.

Ships, like bilious slugs spewing out more of Them,

Who throw rock slabs of Wild stories
Over my white stomach,
"Got to lo...lock them awa...y."

I paste a fat piece of paper over the
Window as They scratch Their Thumbs against it.
I've locked Them out! Now I can forge translucent
Meaning on the foggy anvil!

Schadenfreudian man
Occasionally tries to poke His finger in
My defences, I hear their silence, whispering,
Damned greatest sinners since Satan,
But I'll wait on ages to give me solution.

SLUG-SCAR

On my wrist and leg,
Two crawling slugs,
Eternal slugs
Which will never
Mosey off to devour leaves,
Instead,
Statued to my skin,
They feast on my perfection.
Critter-shitters
Which I can't flick off.

Years later,
Now emaciated worms
Those thin white lines
Defacing my wrist and leg,
Almost forgotten,
But I still feel like a
Squalid backyard -
Put out the salt,
Put out the salt.

SCALPS AND WOUNDS

Stuck in the belly of the moment
like a fetus,
but conscious,
pushing madly,
suffocating suffocation.

Heave!
The second's placental gunk
dripping from me as I emerge from it.

Hoofed light bucks my eye -
scrambling stunned
into the next womb of the millions -
an infinite field of gaping poppies.

But YOU!
You sniggering out in the future
who hold the plot of my
today and tomorrow
in your hands like trophied scalps
hacked from my skull
as I struggle,
throat full of cellophane
in my blunderbuss life.

We're not midgets
rolling about in past's Big Top,
to be gawped at by intrigued families
of a hundred years hence.

If only the future would
shut its beady eye
and allow the present,
allow me,
some privacy -

Future,
get your goddamn axe
out of my life.

HADDOCK

How the sea abhorred that boat -
A liquid lunatic
Kicking and punching,
Swearing and spitting
At the Terrified trawler,
Spit gushing the vessel
Tearing into the fishermen's
Uncovered hands and face -
Already cavernous with the marks
Of previous battles.

The wind clung to the boat,
A monstrous barnacle
Trying to suck
The resistance out
From its flaking green hull,

Gulls buzzed overhead
Hoping to sweep upon dropped fish
But expecting dropped fishermen,
Shell creatures
Hurried from far and wide
To wait impatiently
Under the boat for their
New home to arrive!

Every fish was a
Mammoth tug of war,

41

The sea only relinquishing each
Stretched haddock to the nets
As its hands
Slid off with sweat,
And by God, each of those
Fish was placed in the trough
Like it were a prize pearl
Yanked out of Neptune's
Own hand.

After six hours of
Long war,
Exhausted, the fishermen turned
Back to shore with less fish
Than they were expecting -
But only just less.

THE LAMB

Near by scrapey sheep with miserly tassels of emery
Wire lurching from so violent skin, now here now
Gone polka dancing with the sodomised boughs
Around the Tarpualian Lochs.

This the mothering vista rocking my eyes tenderly in
Her arms, squawking lullabies to the newly seized charge.
Just as quick this view drops from me.

My gaze fires upon an incandescent tree singing off
The shoddy stitches of patchwork nature, and humming
The vibrant countenance of a worm bellied lark.

Uhhh!
You lying shrub with a moulding scrap of newspaper
Spelked on your apex, nothing more than a boiled skeleto
Shaking a branch on a distant hill...
I run clambering through elongated bracken,
Wildly clapping its thorny hands against my side.

I rest against a rock and throttle with loose hands
My pole necked culpability for its whorified acceptance
Of that sweating man's coin.

As the fading day hops dishevelled, screaming gibberish
Over the bitter Lochs, I walk the course of a
Smiling stream...No! A slapped faced, sling armed
Panacea pointing confidently at its own imagined presenc(

43

My eyes' reins are jerked to a lump being coughed from
The streams throat and spat at a moss blown bank to
Which I walk, smashing in the faces of insolent flowers
As they beg me to pull them to freedom!
Crawling over itself,
The stream with quivering fists approaches
This flaccidised lump, smartens up, then
Brutally slaps the face of a mangy dead lamb
Before fleeing away in its utter triumph.

With a twig I prod the corpse of this intriguing
Situation before poking its belly, a horrifying smell shoots
My nose, as a family of dumbfounded maggots
Pack up and leave their tower!

THE TERROR

A repulsive terror
On my skin stuck,
A limpet
Sucking out my juices.
And this is not a limpet
That can be smashed off
With a rock,
For it is a
Ghostly-immateriality,
A mystical mummification
Wrapping me up -
An asphytic condition.
Though I blink the blink of
A dumb fish my tongue
Is nailed to my cruciform mouth
And I am unable to shout.
Before long, the bandages
Wrap about my nose
And mouth
And I back out.
I stand alone,
In a cuboid room
In front of my
Repulsive terror.

PHOTOGRAPH

Picked out in
Black and white,
His image
Swings like a sword
Before my eyes.

This,
The only elucidation
In the World's knot
That he ever was.
His name all but
Scratched off
History's shelf,
Leaving only a
Jagged tearing and
Some hazy lettering.

But one time,
I think he owned Life,
Had it by
The scruff of the neck -
Shoved it in his own direction.

That's most of our
Destinies -
To become a ruined
Photograph.

YOUR LOVE

A lead lump of kiss,
Hooked to my cheek,
A 10-pound fisherman's weight
Pulling my skin into
A bruise as
     I trail on.

As large as the sky,
Your love,
Atlas-weight
On my shoulders,
Burning and crushing
My neck and arms as
     I trail on.

Heavy as a boulder
Stringed to my aorta,
Your love
Pulls my heart
To the floor as
     I trail on.

Your diamond kiss,
Infinite space,
Sucks in my trail
And I walk on
     Burdenless.

TOSSING OFF

The sun tosses off
His coat of clouds
Leaving him standing
Starkers!

Bigness tosses off its smallness,

Noise tosses off its silence,

Happiness tosses off its sadness,

People toss off their clothes,

Hair tosses off sweat,

Umbrellas toss themselves under trains and off cliffs,

Television tosses off its dictatorial grip,

Beaches toss back their welcoming arms,

Fledglings toss off their flightlessness,

Flowers toss off dullness,

And minutes later it starts to rain.

COUNTRYSIDE

A countryside
spread before me like
a spilled cup of coffee.

Lonely trees spouting
forth from the land;
quiet as silence,
they grow.

There that grass;
eye murdering,
so very much of it
a glass of tea.

Then those hills,
grand green tumours
screaming out
"Look at us!
 Look at us!"

Down the carriage
runs a little boy,
not bothering to look
out of the windows.

ASP

Volatile as a land-mine,
The asp, a yellowish wick
Of burning evil,
Its lidless, gummy eyes
Sticking defiantly to everything around,
Saunters between my feet,
Moulded in swagger,
It slithers towards the grass,
I move to one side
Grabbing its image
Tightly as a golden sceptre.

Without warning,
Wildly barks at me,
Its laughing fangs in stitches.

Stunned I pull back
To think on its intentions.
Perhaps the psycho,
Drugged on its own power,
Simply wants to show who's boss -
My puppetish totterings showed I wasn't,

Into the grass it disappears,
Its back-side my final view of it.
I scream abuse at its earless head,
But the victor has notched up
Another carving on its belly-side.

JACK'S FUNERAL

A gaggle of zombies
Life crawling over them like
A blue bottle on a carcass,
Shuffle around the grave.
They mumble mumbles
To each other,
Monosyllabic gone mad.

Haha! I bet Death's nearly
Had a nervous break-down
Trying to get hold of
Old Jack this last week!
I can see them now,
Slagging each other off,
Fighting like cat and dog.

The coffin is lowered down as
A few 'mourners' have a whip round
To buy a carton of cheap tears
From a tear vendor,
Another wraps a yawn in
A cough and looks blankly
At the coffin.

He robbed his life of
Every penny it possessed,
Did our Jack,
And blew it all
On parties!!!

Whoooo-
Those parties,
We would laugh so many tears
We'd dehydrate!

The funeral ends,
The zombies shuffle off
To their graves,
Leaving me and Jack
Watching together
In disbelief.

TUMOUR HEAD

My head -
My gravestone
An ignited piece of
Gelatin,
Puffing and smoking
Away.

Trailing about with
A portable gravestone
Hung from my neck,
Everywhere I move
This remonstrance
At my life
Squealing
"Die! Die!"

O! It's like
I'm one leg
Over Life's fence,
And one leg
Over Death.

TREES

Blood clotted trees
Clumped inside
The veins of the countryside.
Each knotted tree
Congealed around
The clasped,
Praying hands of
The Field.

But the trees
Rupture,
Shaking the meadow
Into convulsions,
Every tree,
A knife stabbing
The countryside's
Thin skin.

A YOUNG PERSON ON DYING

Though life chose to play with me so very short a time,
True Life comes in Death, so my Death is no great crime.
Instead I'll play with Immortality - he's always up for fun
And we'll sit and laugh at Death - that funniest of puns.
For everywhere I ever was, there I'll always be,
But you'll have to drop your human eyes
If you want to gaze on me.
For I'll be your deepest soul and I'll be your deepest brain,
I'll be your deepest comfort during your deepest pain.
But look out into the universe shortly after I die
And concentrate intently on any twinkle in the sky.
I'll be bungee jumping off Pluto, zooming around the sun,
Piggy-backing angels. Yes! Death's a prize hard won.

THE CANCER SLIDE

Pinned down by Fascination's
Burly hands,
Struggle slapped out of me -
"Open Wide" the command
As a litre of Liquidised Question
Is poured down my throat
Drowning my breath like a drunken sailor.
I capitulate.

My Veronicaless Via Dolarosa
To the lab.
With a 400-pound chunk
Of Intrigue
Balanced parrot fashion
On my shoulder,
Whipped by draught
As I push by
Mobs of healers,
Lepers and the possessed
Climbing the stairs -
There it is...
Hitting the landscape of my
Eyes like a meteor
'Onco Lab'

From a smoking tub
A rack is removed
And laid in front of me...

I retch up a mouthful of pungent
Fear
Splattering all over the
Surgeon's typed green file.
And the rack.
Wiping the specks of my
Fear off his face,
The surgeon pulls out a slide
Buttered with the
Me gone mad,
The self
Destroying self.

I was hoping to see
Snarling minute cannibals,
Gobs crammed with me,
Frozen in action inside
Their transparent mausoleum,

Instead,
Sorrow
Ninja-like infiltrates
My brain unseen.
Big blobs amongst many
Smaller blobs,
Reminding me of a child
I once spotted leaving
Nursery...10 feet she must've
Been - a bona fide freak,
Taunted by her class I imagine.
Likewise, these cells' efforts

At blending in
Failed,
The jeers and whispers drove them
Insane...
(I wonder if that girl does
   A Charles Whitman one day?)
The surgeon speaks,
An empty voice jam-packed with words
"You're lucky...eighty percent...tumour...dead."
That means twenty percent of
Them
Were still alive on being removed.
Damn! They put the Auschwitz
Nazis to shame,
Butchering,
Butchering up to the
Last possible moment as
'Chemo' banged on their
Destruction's door.

They would have...ki...killed, me.

Their fundamental
Me-less-ness
Shocks my empathy
Out of its skin.
My memory's eyes
Fill with tears
At what they put through me.

A YOUNG POET'S DEATH

Locked as
Treasure in his twenty-year-old
Chest,
He shouts and wails,
Urging Age,
That great buzzard
To sweep upon him
And drop him
Into a future.

Instead it flies
Above a gaping grave
And plummets him,
Bound in his metal chest,
Down a six foot hole -
A straight shoot to
Pristine Death.

O! Those finger-tips,
Each a screaming madman,
Choler full
With the information,
The advice he might have
Released onto the World's brain.
Now they claw against his metal chest
And tear into his starving belly.

A ROSE SEQUENCE

The rose
Is nature's imitation of
An Angel -
Those who,
Millions of years ago
Implored God to show
Mercy on blandness.
Thus came about
The Created uncreatable.

The rose,
Hero-worshipped by
The little daisy,
The bane of the weed.
Beautifier of grass,
A stud to the lady flowers!
And the super-model of plants!

The rose
I see from my window
Has blossomed
Beauty into divinity,
Has become an
Intense aberration of
Orthodox colour,
Outshining the noon light
To a humiliated
Pitch black.

The rose
Which there wilts
In a florist's bucket
And once freely danced
To the Sun's song,
Will probably be bought by
An adulterous spouse
Or become one of the lover's
Tools to crack the rock
Of an unreceptive heart!
But soon its beauty
Will drop off in tears,
And in the bin will go
The rose.

PARALYSED

It feels-as-if-my brain
Is-shagging-pain,
As I lie here
In this murky place.
I am attached to
An I.V. drip pumping
Raw shit
Into my veins.
Oh my God,
Nothing moves.

I'm in such agony.

SUN

Declared by God,
This act of gold,
This Sun
Burns the Day
To a lump of charcoal
In the middle of a bleak room.

I creep about
The Earth on
Motherish,
Night-time tip-toes,
Aware that any
Unguarded footstep
Could start an inferno.

I watch the Earth
Bleed fire from its
Every pore,
This yellow-red blood
Locked inside everything,
Waiting for
The right moment
To leap out.

Still I feel the Sun
Lay into my skin
And O! How I dread
Breathing.

CARVING A PIETA FROM AN ATOM

Throw heaven and earth into a sack
And carry it always on your back.
Go up to god's black eye, spit in his face, say goodbye,
Take the devil by his balls and bounce him off
Hell's slimy walls!
Roll death on your palm,
Touch it, stroke it without alarm,
Ride your life the buckshot horse,
Whipping it always to stay on course.
Do in a second an hour's job -
From time you must begin to rob.
Stand on stacked-up years to touch eternity -
Your home in all certainty.
Scale Everest with a smile,
Scaling mountains is no great trail!
Carve a Pieta from an atom.........